Jide writes from amazing insight and understanding. This book is an excellent primer on the nuances of spiritual formation that are becoming lost – quite unfortunately – in these days of mass superficiality. I recommend it without reservation to anyone serious about growing up spiritually.

– **Akin Akinrinmade**, Founder, Energeo, South Africa

❖ ❖ ❖ ❖ ❖ ❖ ❖

What You're Going to Be When You Grow Up *is a powerful, biblical, equipping tool that will empower any believer to become what they are meant to become as a disciple in Christ! Read it! Apply it!*

– **Paul Becker**, President/Founder, Dynamic Church Planting International, USA

❖ ❖ ❖ ❖ ❖ ❖ ❖

This is an excellent piece – a vital reminder of what the gospel is and what our conduct as ambassadors and custodians of it should be. Its simplicity and the illustrations contained therein, bring clarity and make for practical application. Thank you Jide for such a powerful message that is needed in today's church. Too many adulterations of the gospel abound which belie and undo the selfless sacrifices of those who gave their lives, and counted all things but dung so they could win Christ. I highly recommend this book. Get ready to be challenged to live the higher life!

– **Inyang Okutinyang**, Pastor, Faith Impact Church, Nigeria

Precise, concise and plain speaking. Jide Lawal writes from the heart and calls us back to true biblical Christianity. When I grow up, I want to be like Jesus! This thought provoking read encourages and inspires me to be well on my way!

– **Toyin Okutinyang**, Pastor, Faith Impact Church, Nigeria

◆ ◆ ◆ ◆ ◆ ◆ ◆

Without question, the singular and perennial objective for every believer, right from the moment of the New Birth, is true spiritual growth. Sadly, there appears to be a dearth of resources on this critical subject. In this book, the author paints a beautiful biblical portrait of the essence of spiritual growth and shows how easy it can be to predict one's future.

– **Ire Ogunsina**, Pastor, Epiphany Church, Birmingham, UK.

◆ ◆ ◆ ◆ ◆ ◆ ◆

If you are a Christian and want a book to set you on the right track for spiritual growth and keep you on it – this is it. I highly recommend you read it periodically – at least twice a year. It will help shape and sharpen your perspective of why you are here and what you are here for. It will give a deeper and clearer meaning to your Christian race.

– **Kemi Williams**, Minister/Founder, The Higher Ground Ministries, Nigeria.

What You're Going To Be When You Grow Up

What You're Going To Be When You Grow Up

JIDE LAWAL

InnerSeede Media ● Lagos, Nigeria

Contents

Foreword

I have known Jide quite closely for several years. His passion for the things of God is remarkable, and his heart to see the truths of God's Word clearly expressed is undeniable. I am impressed by his desire to see us as believers take our place in Christ .

God's plan is for every believer to grow up in Christ, and to walk in the fullness of God's plans and purposes for his or her life. A lot of the problems we experience in the Body of Christ today would be solved if believers were to mature in Him. Any parent would be heart-broken to have a child who isn't growing up mentally or physically. In the same way, our Father is never pleased when any-one of His children isn't growing spiritually. Nothing can be sub-stituted for spiritual growth.

There's a clarion call in this book that's for this hour, and that call is for believers to get back to native Christianity with a fresh ded-ication to the gospel in its simplicity. I believe you will be edified, encouraged and challenged to go all out for God and mature in your walk with Him as a result of reading this masterpiece.

Tokunbo Adejuwon
National Director,
Rhema Bible Training Centre,
Abuja, Nigeria.

1. What Are You Going to Be When You Grow Up?

A few years ago, I wrote an article titled "Spiritual Growth". I don't remember much of what I wrote, but I recall I struggled with putting down a definition for spiritual growth. What is spiritual growth? What does it mean to say the believer in Christ is growing or has matured spiritually?

I still don't have a definition that satisfies me, but while studying what the Bible has to say on the subject, I discovered that the Bible has a lot of content describing what the believer who has grown spiritually is like.

In Nigeria, we have an expression that we use colloquially – "I want to be like you when I grow up". We say this to express admiration for someone who we feel has made remarkable achievement or progress in some endeavour or the other, and to express a desire to do the same.

2 Corinthians 5

17 Therefore if any man be in Christ, he is a new creation: old things are passed away; behold, all things are become new.

The Bible introduces the believer to us as a "New Creature". The New Creature is blood-bought[1] and blood-washed[2], delivered from the power of darkness[3], made righteous[4], justified[5] and sanctified[6], ransomed and redeemed[7] by the sacrifice of the Son of God Himself. He is filled with the Spirit of God[8], is endued with the power of God[9], and is standing in the grace of God[10]. He is God's workmanship[11], the crowning jewel of God's creation. He is an heir of God and a joint-heir with Jesus Christ[12]. He is created in righteousness and true holiness[13]. He is sealed with the Holy Spirit of promise[14]. He is authorised to use the Name of Jesus in prayer[15]. He has been brought into fellowship with the Father and the Son and the Holy Spirit[16]. He has received the power to become a son of God[17]. He is blessed with all spiritual blessings in heavenly places[18]. He has received all things that pertain to life and godli-

1. 1 Peter 1:19
2. Revelation 1:5
3. Colossians 1:13
4. 2 Corinthians 5:21
5. Romans 5:1
6. 1 Corinthians 6:11
7. 1 Peter 1:18
8. Titus 3:5-6
9. Luke 24:49, Acts 1:8
10. Romans 5:1-2
11. Ephesians 2:10
12. Romans 8:17
13. Ephesians 4:24
14. Ephesians 1:13
15. John 16:24
16. 1 John 1:3, 2 Corinthians 13:14
17. John 1:12
18. Ephesians 1:3

ness[19]. He is now a partaker of God's divine nature[20]. He is seated in heavenly places in Christ Jesus[21]. He was once under God's wrath[22], but is now accepted in the beloved[23]. He was once on his way to hell, but is now a citizen of heaven[24]. His sins have been remitted[25]. He has been saved by the washing of regeneration, and the renewing of the Holy Ghost[26]. He is joined to the Lord in one spirit[27].

He's not the person he used to be. He no longer has the nature of the devil; he now has the nature of God!

During the earthly ministry of Jesus, His disciples asked, "What manner of man is this?" Well, Jesus died and rose again, so that we would become the manner of man He was! He shared our human nature so that we could share His divine nature!

God's Expectation is Growth

The Bible tells us that the New Creature is expected to grow. It is this growth, whatever it is, that is referred to as Spiritual Growth.

Ephesians 4
14 That we from now on be no more children, tossed to and fro, and carried about with every wind of doctrine, by the sleight of men, and cunning craftiness, by which they lie in wait to deceive;

19. 2 Peter 1:3
20. 2 Peter 1:4
21. Ephesians 2:6
22. John 3:36, Romans 1:18
23. Ephesians 1:6
24. Philippians 3:20
25. Ephesians 1:7, Colossians 1:14
26. Titus 3:5
27. 1 Corinthians 6:17

15 But speaking the truth in love, may grow up into him in all things, who is the head, even Christ:

1 Peter 2
2 As newborn babes, desire the pure milk of the word, that you may grow thereby:

Many other books have attempted to define Spiritual Growth, and the process by which it occurs. This book does not intend to do that. Instead, we will describe what the New Creature will be like when he has come to maturity. A good picture of what we will be when we mature will help us. It will challenge us, inspire us, and keep a picture of our goal before us. It will motivate us to invest the time and effort in the things of God that we require in order to ensure that we keep growing.

2. **Metaphors of the Mystery**

Colossians 1

*26 Even **the mystery** which has been hid from ages and from generations, but now is made manifest to his saints:*

*27 To whom God would make known what is the riches of the glory of **this mystery** among the Gentiles; which is Christ in you, the hope of glory:*

28 Whom we preach, warning every man, and teaching every man in all wisdom; that we may present every man perfect in Christ Jesus:

29 For which I also labor, striving according to his working, who works in me mightily.

In his epistles, Paul consistently writes about something he calls "a mystery", or sometimes "the mystery". He uses this word in the way we would normally use the word "secret". In fact, some modern versions use the word "secret" rather than "mystery".

We normally use the word "mystery" to mean something difficult or impossible to understand, perhaps associated with the dark arts.

Because the translators of the King James Version chose to use the word "mystery" (it might have been appropriate for their time in 1611), many have pounced on that word to suggest that the things of God are difficult or impossible to understand. Some have even suggested that God Himself is mysterious, or that He does mysterious things. We hear some clergymen declare with all gravity, "God works in mysterious ways, His wonders to perform".

But we start to get a better understanding of what Paul was talking about when we realise that he means "a secret", not "a mystery". For example, if I asked you to tell me what I gave my wife as a wedding gift, you probably wouldn't know. But it would be a secret to you, not a mystery. And once I tell you I gave her a Bible, you would realise that it was never mysterious, it was just a secret you didn't know. If you didn't watch a particular sports event yesterday and hadn't gotten any news about it, the result would be a secret, not a mystery. Once I told you the score, it would neither be a secret nor a mystery.

In the same way, there is nothing mysterious about what the King James Version translators rendered as "the mystery which hath been hid from ages and from generations". It wasn't so mysterious after all; it was merely a secret. And like many other secrets, once it is revealed, it is possible to understand.

Television would look mysterious, perhaps like dark magic to someone who has never had access to modern comforts. They would wonder how 6-inch sized people were inserted into the screen. But today it is no longer so, even to illiterate people who have access to electricity and other modern comforts. They may not understand the technology that makes television possible, but they know that there are television stations where people work and the moving images are captured and broadcast. There was never anything mysterious about it – the technology is a secret which is freely revealed to anyone who can spare the time and resources to go to school to learn all about it.

What Was Paul's Secret?

If we're ready to take out time to study, we can learn the secret that Paul was talking about! He states it so plainly:

> 1. The secret was hidden from previous generations, but is now revealed to the saints (all believers in Christ).
> 2. The secret is "Christ in you, the hope of glory".
> 3. He teaches and preaches so that he would be able to "present every man **perfect** in Christ". The word "perfect" here is better translated as "complete, grown up or mature".

If you were to pay me a visit, you would probably show no surprise when you notice that I own a television set. You probably have one too, and have watched television all your life. Unless there was something remarkable about the television set or it was showing a programme you had particular interest in, you'd probably ignore the television set and concentrate on visiting with me.

This is the same way many Christians treat the secret which Paul is talking about. Much like people who have never had access to modern technology would be entranced by a television set, they're interested to read about "a mystery". They would want to listen to a preacher who says, "God has revealed a mystery to me which I want to share with the Body of Christ". But if someone else were to say, "I want to teach on 'Christ in you, the Hope of Glory'", they may not show too much interest, the same way you would not show any interest in my television set. You're used to television; you've come to take it for granted.

Let's Pay Attention to Paul's Secret

We need to go back and pay attention to Paul's "secret". He states clearly that it is what he teaches and preaches, so as to be able to present every man "complete, grown up or mature" in Christ. Peter said we were to desire the sincere milk of the Word so that we would grow. If we want to know what the New Creature is going to be like when he is grown, then we need to pay attention to Paul's secret and make the most of it.

Paul declares that the reason why some Christians were put in ministry offices is for "the perfecting", or "the growth and maturity" of all believers.

Ephesians 4
11 And he gave some, apostles; and some, prophets; and some, evangelists; and some, pastors and teachers;
12 For the perfecting of the saints, for the work of the ministry, for the edifying of the body of Christ:
13 Till we all come in the unity of the faith, and of the knowledge of the Son of God, unto a perfect man, unto the measure of the stature of the fullness of Christ:
14 That we from now on be no more children, tossed to and fro, and carried about with every wind of doctrine, by the sleight of men, and cunning craftiness, by which they lie in wait to deceive;
*15 But speaking the truth in love, may **grow up into him** in all things, who is the head, even Christ:*

To the Colossians, he says that he was teaching and preaching to present every man "complete, grown up or mature" in Christ. To the Ephesians, he says that apostles, prophets, evangelists, pastors and teachers are given so that we would all come in the unity of the faith and the knowledge of the Son of God "unto a complete, grown up or mature" man. The goal is to present **every man** mature in Christ.

What is a Metaphor?

A metaphor is a figure of speech in which a word or phrase that literally denotes one kind of object or idea, is used in place of another to suggest a likeness or analogy between them[1]. For example, I could look at someone and say, "You're just a clown!" This doesn't necessarily mean that I consider them to be a man or a woman who earns a living by making little children laugh and getting paid for it. It means that I think they are very much *like* a clown in that they make me laugh, the same way actual clowns do.

There are quite a number of metaphors in the New Testament which are presented as an ideal for the believer in Christ to aspire to. They are used to represent the character traits and preoccupations we would observe in a believer who has grown.

Not every possible trait of these metaphors should be applied to the believer – we should understand the context in which they were used. In fact, without an understanding of the context, the metaphors would at once be contradictory! For example, the believer is presented at once as a king and as a servant! In appraising this, we must understand the ways in which the believer is supposed to be *like* a king, and the ways in which he is supposed to be *like* a servant.

---

1. Merriam-Webster Online Dictionary © 2015 Merriam-Webster, Inc.

These metaphors reveal what we're going to be *like* when we grow up!

3. **The Faithful Steward**

1 Corinthians 4
1 Let a man so account of us, as of the ministers of Christ, and stewards of the mysteries of God.
2 Moreover it is required in stewards, that a man be found faithful.

A steward is someone who manages household affairs in a subordinate position, on behalf of someone else. He has a master or a mistress who typically owns the household. Usually a steward must serve 3 classes of people:

> 1. Serve his master.
> 2. Serve the other members of the household, such as the master's family.
> 3. Serve his master's guests.

Paul tells us here that to be good Christians, we must be faithful stewards. This isn't something that we automatically received in the New Birth; we must make a conscious effort to attain to it.

Just like a typical steward, we must serve 3 different classes of people:

1. God, our master.
2. Other believers – members of the Body of Christ.
3. Unbelievers.

And we must serve them faithfully!

Personally, I've observed many people who want to serve God. They're zealous. They usually start out with good intentions. They truly want to serve; they want to be a blessing to others. But it's somewhat hard to describe them as faithful.

How do I reach this conclusion? Very easy. I don't have a steward, but if I did, I wouldn't want a steward that has the same attitude to my household that these believers have to God's household.

They serve on their own terms. They come and go as they please. They serve joyfully when they're happy, and when they're unhappy, they show up moody or don't show up at all. They have an unhealthy sense of rivalry and competition with other stewards. They seem to seek to build their own empires, rather than make God's Kingdom their priority. People like them are not unique to our day – Paul knew such people too!

Philippians 1
15 Some indeed preach Christ even of envy and strife; and some also of good will:
16 The one preach Christ out of contention, not sincerely, supposing to add affliction to my bonds:

You Will Render an Account of Your Service to God

We must always remember that we will one day render an account of our service to God Himself. Would you want a steward that acts without a sense of duty, not keeping in mind the fact that you would be dissatisfied with his poor performance?

2 Corinthians 5
9 Therefore we labor, that, whether present or absent, we may be accepted of him.
10 For we must all appear before the judgment seat of Christ; that everyone may be recompensed for the things done in his body, according to what he has done, whether it be good or bad.

Some Christians decide which of God's children they like and let that show up in their service. Some show a fawning adulation to the rich, and ignore the poor. Would you want a steward that treats some of your children poorly and treats the others nicely? Or one that was polite to some of your guests and discourteous to the others?

1 Timothy 5
*21 I charge you before God, and the Lord Jesus Christ, and the elect angels, that you observe these things without preferring one before another, **doing nothing by partiality**.*

James 2
*1 My brethren, have not the faith of our Lord Jesus Christ, the Lord of glory, **with respect of persons**.*

A Steward of His Secrets

As a steward, you're primarily a custodian of the mysteries, or as we have learnt, the secrets of God. I have read authors who point out that God has placed us as stewards, and we should manage our time, our money, our bodies and our secular vocations wisely.

I agree. We ought to be good managers of these things. But the reason we need to manage these things very well is because we are stewards of God's secrets!

1 Corinthians 4
1 Let a man so account of us, as of the ministers of Christ, and stewards of the mysteries of God.

Of what use is good time management and good financial management in a steward who is serving a poisonous meal? Of what use is good time management and good financial management in a church that is teaching false doctrine? Some ignore God's instructions to only feed His family with sound doctrine, and give them whatever diet they prefer to feed on. Would you want that kind of steward feeding your own children?

2 Timothy 4
1 I charge you therefore before God, and the Lord Jesus Christ, who shall judge the living and the dead at his appearing and his kingdom;
2 Preach the word; be diligent in season, out of season; reprove, rebuke, exhort with all longsuffering and doctrine.
*3 For the time will come when **they will not endure sound doctrine**; but **after their own lusts** shall they draw to themselves teachers, **having itching ears**;*
4 And they shall turn away their ears from the truth, and shall be turned unto myths.

Matthew 24
45 Who then is a faithful and wise servant, whom his lord has made ruler over his household, to give them food at the proper time?

46 Blessed is that servant, whom his lord when he comes shall find so doing.

Be Faithful in Little Things

A common mistake is to think that you do not need to be faithful when you're just starting out, or that only believers who are in charge of very large ministries need to be faithful. No, the Lord wants each and every one of us to be faithful! In fact, He tells us that faithfulness in little things usually precedes faithfulness in greater things, and that unfaithfulness in little things suggests that you will also be unfaithful in greater things.

Luke 16
10 He that is faithful in that which is least is faithful also in much: and he that is unjust in the least is unjust also in much.
11 If therefore you have not been faithful in the unrighteous mammon, who will commit to your trust the true riches?
12 And if you have not been faithful in that which is another man's, who shall give you that which is your own?

Now, what does Jesus consider to be little things? Notice He speaks about unrighteous mammon (money) as being of inferior value to "the true riches". I have observed that many believers who prove unfaithful in managing money or who cannot be trusted with it also prove to be unfaithful in the things of God.

Paul and Barnabas are examples of men who were promoted to greater things in ministry after they had first been proved in the area of handling money.

Acts 11
27 And in these days came prophets from Jerusalem unto Antioch.
28 And there stood up one of them named Agabus, and signified by

the Spirit that there should be great famine throughout all the world: which came to pass in the days of Claudius Caesar.

29 Then the disciples, every man according to his ability, determined to send relief unto the brethren who dwelt in Judea:

30 Which also they did, and sent it to the elders by the hands of Barnabas and Saul.

Acts 12

25 And Barnabas and Saul returned from Jerusalem, when they had fulfilled their ministry, and took with them John, whose surname was Mark.

Acts 13

1 Now there were in the church that was at Antioch certain prophets and teachers; as Barnabas, and Simeon that was called Niger, and Lucius of Cyrene, and Manaen, who had been brought up with Herod the tetrarch, and Saul.

2 As they ministered to the Lord, and fasted, the Holy Spirit said, Separate me Barnabas and Saul for the work to which I have called them.

3 And when they had fasted and prayed, and laid their hands on them, they sent them away.

Paul and Barnabas could be trusted to become apostles and be sent on a difficult missionary journey where their faithfulness would be sorely tried. They had been on a journey before where they had been in charge of money, and they proved faithful.

Money isn't the only "little thing". Other examples are our use of time, and our use of our bodies. If we are unfaithful to the Lord in these, we are unlikely to be faithful in greater things.

I wish I could say I've always been faithful. I wish I could say I've never fallen short of my Lord's expectations. I can't. Perhaps you can, perhaps you can't.

But we can all purpose to be faithful, going forward. We can all purpose to grow up in Him and prove to be good stewards to our Lord! There is a great need in the Body of Christ today for men and women who will be faithful, constrained by His love.

2 Corinthians 5
14 For the love of Christ constrains us; because we thus judge, that if one died for all, then were all dead:
15 And that he died for all, that they who live should no longer live unto themselves, but unto him who died for them, and rose again.

4. **The Suffering Ambassador**

2 Corinthians 5
20 Now then we are ambassadors for Christ, as though God did beseech you by us: we pray you on Christ's behalf, be reconciled to God.

Sometimes we have words used in the Bible which are no longer in common use in modern times. An example of such a word is "seer".

1 Samuel 9
9 (Formerly in Israel, when a man went to inquire of God, thus he spoke, Come, and let us go to the seer: for he that is now called a Prophet was formerly called a Seer.)

Today we rarely have anyone referred to as a seer, whether in a Christian context or not.

But we have many words which were in use in Bible times, and are still being used today. Where we see these words, we should be careful to see if there is any difference in the way they are used in the Bible, and the way they are used in the world today. An example of such a word is "ambassador", as used by Paul to describe himself.

Paul simply uses the word "ambassador" to mean "representative". He does not use it to connote a high office and the perks and honours that go along with it such as we understand the office of an ambassador to mean today. There were ambassadors in Paul's day who were fêted and celebrated like ambassadors are today, but as we will see, he wasn't one of that kind.

Ephesians 6
19 And for me, that utterance may be given unto me, that I may open my mouth boldly, to make known the mystery of the gospel,
*20 For which **I am an ambassador in bonds**: that in this I may speak boldly, as I ought to speak.*

Paul describes himself as **an ambassador in bonds**! He represents the kingdom of Christ, but this service has earned him chains!

I have heard ideas and sentiments that run like this among Christians – "Do ambassadors live with the rich, or with the poor? Would the United States ambassador to Nigeria have his home in the high-end residential areas of the capital of Nigeria, or in the slums? As Christ's ambassadors, we should enjoy the best this world has to offer, because we come from the richest of kingdoms!"

To be frank, this opinion is based on a misunderstanding of the word "ambassador" as used in the Bible, as well as ignorance of our calling. We are Christ's ambassadors, but our kingdom is at war with the kingdoms of this world. We are ambassadors in hostile territory. We are not here to enjoy the pleasures of this world. We have a mission and an assignment which will always put us in conflict with the systems of this world.

John 16
33 These things I have spoken unto you, that in me you might have peace. In the world you shall have tribulation: but be of good cheer; I have overcome the world.

John 15
19 If you were of the world, the world would love its own: but because you are not of the world, but I have chosen you out of the world, therefore the world hates you.

When we grow up spiritually, part of our maturity will be the realization that there is no higher honour that this world can afford, than to be acclaimed as one who suffered for the sake of the gospel. **There is no higher honour that we can receive in this world, than to be distinguished for our sufferings for the cause of Christ.** To be known as a Suffering Ambassador is a privilege that we will all crave when we grow up in Him.

You do not need to go looking for persecution – it will come looking for you if you will simply live a godly life.

2 Timothy 3
12 Yea, and all that will live godly in Christ Jesus shall suffer persecution.

Our lifestyles, if they are godly, will attract persecution. We will not be able to avoid or escape the opposition of the ungodly unless we live our lives in treasonous compromise with the systems of this world.

Acts 5
40 And to him they agreed: and when they had called the apostles, **and beaten them**, *they commanded that they should not speak in the name of Jesus, and let them go.*
41 And they departed from the presence of the council, **rejoicing that they were counted worthy to suffer shame for his name.**

The apostles rejoiced after being beaten – because they were happy that they had been counted worthy to suffer shame for the Name of Christ! This attitude to persecution is rare in our days. In our day, many men and women who profess the cause of Christ no longer count it all joy to suffer for Him. We are more likely to be found murmuring, complaining and expressing anger when we have to put up with the least bit of indignities for the sake of our Christianity. We start a pity-party and engage the Press to shed light on our plight. We attempt to gain the moral high ground and denounce the persecutors as being evil. We get in touch with human rights groups and engage lawyers to seek legal redress. We do everything except what the apostles did – rejoice!

I don't think it's wrong to seek legal redress or to try to have your rights enforced when you're being persecuted for Christ's sake. Paul certainly seemed to appeal to the law in his day[1]. But we must never lose our joy or become bitter or seek to be avenged.

Colossians 1
24 Who now rejoice in my sufferings for you, and fill up that which is behind of the afflictions of Christ in my flesh for his body's sake, which is the church:

Hebrews 10
32 But call to remembrance the former days, in which, after you were

---

1. Acts 22:24-29, Acts 25:11, Acts 28:19

illuminated, you endured a great fight with afflictions;
*33 Partly, while you were made a public display both by reproaches
and afflictions; and partly, while you became companions of them
that were so used.*
*34 For you had compassion on me in my bonds, **and took joyfully
the spoiling of your goods**, knowing in yourselves that you have
in heaven a better and an enduring possession.*

Are You Willing to Suffer for Christ's Sake?

If you cannot suffer shame for the cause of Christ, how would you
be able to endure greater suffering? Many believers do not identify
openly with Christ in some situations for fear of a loss of societal
standing, for fear of a loss of financial benefits, for fear of a nega-
tive opinion from others. This has led to a culture of Political Cor-
rectness, even in the Church.

2 Corinthians 1
*3 Blessed be God, even the Father of our Lord Jesus Christ, the Father
of mercies, and the God of all comfort;*
*4 Who comforts us in all our tribulation, that we may be able to com-
fort them who are in any trouble, by the comfort with which we ourselves are comforted of God.*
*5 For as the sufferings of Christ abound in us, so our consolation also
abounds by Christ.*
*6 **And whether we be afflicted, it is for your consolation and
salvation**, which is effectual in the enduring of the same sufferings
which we also suffer: or whether we be comforted, it is for your consolation and salvation.*
*7 And our hope of you is steadfast, knowing, that as you are partak-
ers of the sufferings, so shall you be also of the consolation.*
8 For we would not, brethren, have you ignorant of our trouble which

came to us in Asia, that we were pressed out of measure, above strength, so that we despaired even of life:

Christianity as preached in our times, is so different from the way it was in the first century that the words "faith" and "tribulation" are rarely used together as they are in these verses:

Acts 14
21 And when they had preached the gospel to that city, and had taught many, they returned again to Lystra, and to Iconium, and Antioch,
*22 Confirming the souls of the disciples, and exhorting them to **continue in the faith**, and that **we must through much tribulation enter into the kingdom of God.***

If the first charge in the verse above is important, then the second one is important, too. In fact, there is a correlation to them. To continue in the faith is to risk enduring much tribulation.

Today, the work of God has suffered in the hands of men and women who suppose that "gain is godliness"[2]. Their god is their belly, their glory is their shame, they mind earthly things. They have brought the ministry into disrepute with their greed and avarice[3]. When they grow up, they will understand their calling as one to suffer for the sake of the Gospel.

1 Peter 2
19 For this is commendable, if a man for conscience toward God endures grief, suffering wrongfully.
*20 For what glory is it, if, when you be buffeted for your faults, you shall take it patiently? but if, when you do well, and suffer for it, **you***

2. 1 Timothy 6:5
3. Philippians 3:19

take it patiently, this is commendable with God.

*21 For even to this were you called: because Christ also suffered for us, **leaving us an example**, that you should follow his steps:*

Paul's Testimony about His Sufferings

Let us consider the testimony of Paul about his sufferings. This will help us understand his claim that he is "an ambassador in bonds".

2 Corinthians 11

*23 Are they ministers of Christ? (I speak as a fool) I am more; in labors more abundant, in stripes beyond measure, in prisons more frequent, **in deaths often**.*

24 Of the Jews five times received I forty stripes less one.

25 Three times was I beaten with rods, once was I stoned, three times I suffered shipwreck, a night and a day I have been in the deep;

26 In journeys often, in perils of waters, in perils of robbers, in perils by my own countrymen, in perils by the Gentiles, in perils in the city, in perils in the wilderness, in perils in the sea, in perils among false brethren;

27 In weariness and painfulness, in watchings often, in hunger and thirst, in fastings often, in cold and nakedness.

*28 Besides those things that are outside, **that which comes upon me daily, the care of all the churches**.*

Paul declares here that he had died many times! Does this mean he actually died and was resurrected from the dead many times? Maybe, maybe not. I think this is a figurative way of saying he had laid down his life many times, and was only spared by the mercy of God.

Acts 14

19 And there came there certain Jews from Antioch and Iconium, who

persuaded the people, and, having stoned Paul, drew him out of the city, supposing he had been dead.
20 However, as the disciples stood round about him, he rose up, and came into the city: and the next day he departed with Barnabas to Derbe.

When a mob tries to murder you and they stone you and leave you for dead, you're probably very close to dead, anyway. You're unlikely to be just a little worse for wear.

In spite of all the sufferings Paul went through, his prime preoccupation was still "the care of all the churches". Our obsession in our day and time seems to be with ourselves and our needs. We seem to appreciate all the blessings and the provision of God only with respect to how they meet our needs.

Philippians 2
21 For all seek their own, not the things which are Jesus Christ's.

There is nothing wrong with having our needs met. Our God is a loving Father and He wants us to be well provided for. However, it is obvious that the work of God will suffer in our hands unless we are ready to sacrifice for it.

Philippians 2
17 Yea, and if I be offered upon the sacrifice and service of your faith, I joy, and rejoice with you all.
18 For the same cause also do you joy, and rejoice with me.

Colossians 1
24 Who now rejoice in my sufferings for you, and fill up that which is behind of the afflictions of Christ in my flesh for his body's sake, which is the church:

Without our sufferings for the sake of the gospel, Christ's suffering may end up being in vain for some people. Unless we go to tell them what He did on the cross, His sacrifice there may as well not have happened for them.

Jesus taught about the danger of loving our lives, but this is a message rarely repeated by preachers today.

Luke 14
26 If any man come to me, and hate not his father, and mother, and wife, and children, and brothers, and sisters, yea, and his own life also, he cannot be my disciple.
27 And whosoever does not bear his cross, and come after me, cannot be my disciple.

Revelation 12
*11 And they overcame him by the blood of the Lamb, and by the word of their testimony; and **they loved not their lives unto death**.*

When we grow up, we will sacrifice our lives willingly for the gospel. We will lose our fear, and celebrate the freedom from the fear of death that Jesus died to give to us.

Hebrews 2
14 Since then the children are partakers of flesh and blood, he also himself likewise took part of the same; that through death he might destroy him that had the power of death, that is, the devil;
*15 And **deliver them** who through fear of death were all their lifetime subject to bondage.*

5. **The Travailing Father**

Galatians 4
19 My little children, of whom I travail in birth again until Christ be formed in you,

Paul planted the churches in Galatia. They were the direct result of his ministry. The Acts of the Apostles records that he visited them twice[1]. It is not clear whether the Letter to the Galatians was written to them after his first visit, or after the second.

What is clear, however, is that he wrote this letter to them after the churches of Galatia had entertained false teachers who had caused them to stray from the truth into error. Paul had preached the Gospel to them, and they had gotten born again, after the death and the resurrection of Jesus had been validated before their eyes via signs and wonders[2]. Paul had invested time, labour, prayers,

1. Acts 16:6, Acts 18:23
2. Galatians 3:1

etc. on them, only to hear that they had received "another gospel". And what was his response?

He declared his readiness to "travail again in birth". This metaphor is taken from human reproduction. He states that he would labour again as though he were a woman trying to birth a baby. What a great expression of love!

One of the highest expressions of human sacrifice is the great pain, great risk, and great stress that women go through to give birth. And she would be a Queen among mothers who says to her child, "Due to no fault of mine you are in some bad situation now, but I am ready to go through the dangers and pain of childbirth for you again if it would somehow save you from your troubles".

This was Paul's attitude. This was Paul's conclusion on the matter. He was ready to travail in birth again. He was ready to do the work all over again.

1 Thessalonians 2
1 For yourselves, brethren, know our visit unto you, that it was not in vain:
2 But even after we had suffered before, and were shamefully treated, as you know, at Philippi, we were bold in our God to speak unto you the gospel of God with much opposition.
3 For our exhortation was not of deceit, nor of uncleanness, nor in guile:
4 But as we were allowed of God to be put in trust with the gospel, even so we speak; not as pleasing men, but God, who tests our hearts.
*5 For **neither at any time used we flattering words**, as you know, nor **a cloak of covetousness**; God is witness:*
6 Nor of men sought we glory, neither of you, nor yet of others, when we might have been burdensome, as the apostles of Christ.

7 But we were gentle among you, even as a nurse cherishes her children:

*8 So being affectionately desirous of you, **we were willing to have imparted unto you**, not the gospel of God only, **but also our own souls**, because you were dear unto us.*

*9 For you remember, brethren, **our labor and travail**: for laboring night and day, because we would not be a burden unto any of you, we preached unto you the gospel of God.*

10 You are witnesses, and God also, how holy and just and unblamable was our behavior among you that believe:

*11 As you know how we exhorted and encouraged and charged every one of you, **as a father does his children**,*

12 That you would walk worthy of God, who has called you unto his kingdom and glory.

Don't Be Quick to Give Up on Others

There is something about not being quick to give up on others that is a sign of spiritual maturity. And while we're on the subject, we need to concede that some people are very easy to give up on!

I wish I had known this, years ago, perhaps I wouldn't have given up on some people. And I wish some other people had known it too, perhaps they wouldn't have given up on me!

When believers misbehave, when they refuse to walk in the truth, when they act unseemly, when they backslide, we ought to always remember that God has called them to His kingdom and glory, and help to restore them to the faith.

3 John
4 I have no greater joy than to hear that my children walk in truth.

We should have no greater joy than seeing believers walking in the truth, and nothing should cause us more pain than seeing them out of the Way. This idea is presented in many ways and forms all over the epistles.

Romans 9
1 I say the truth in Christ, I lie not, my conscience also bearing me witness in the Holy Spirit,
2 That I have great heaviness and continual sorrow in my heart.
*3 **For I could wish that I myself were accursed from Christ for my brethren**, my kinsmen according to the flesh:*
4 Who are Israelites; to whom pertains the adoption, and the glory, and the covenants, and the giving of the law, and the service of God, and the promises;

This expression of the love of God in Paul's heart for his brethren is quite startling! He could wish that he were accursed from Christ for their sakes! And he was talking about the Jews, the same people who had persecuted him relentlessly everywhere he went in the course of his ministry! Paul says he wouldn't think it too much for him to suffer eternal damnation, if that's what it would take for the Israelites to receive eternal salvation!

Whenever I hear of church leaders cursing a church member, I never even bother to find out what the church member has done to deserve such treatment. I know we are dealing with a church leader who himself is not yet a Travailing Father. When he grows up, he will leave childish things.

When we grow up, we will share Paul's passion for the lost. The same burden for the salvation (or restoration to the faith) of those around us will cause us to consider whatever sacrifices we may need to make for their sake insignificant.

Ephesians 3
*13 Therefore I desire that you faint not at **my tribulations for you**, which is your glory.*

Colossians 1
28 Whom we preach, warning every man, and teaching every man in all wisdom; that we may present every man perfect in Christ Jesus: 29 For which I also labor, striving according to his working, who works in me mightily.

Never Let Them Forget

Many times, our sacrifices for the saints will not be as dramatic and as extreme as those of Jesus or of Paul. Sometimes it will be in an area so subtle that we tend to overlook it. It could be in the area of reminding believers of the things we all ought to always keep in mind as Christians.

Philippians 3
*1 Finally, my brethren, rejoice in the Lord. **To write the same things to you**, to me indeed is not troublesome, but for you it is safe.*

1 Timothy 4
*6 If you put the brethren **in remembrance of these things**, you shall be a good minister of Jesus Christ, nourished up in the words of faith and of good doctrine, which you have attained.*

2 Peter 1
*12 Therefore I will not be negligent to put you **always in remembrance of these things**, though you know them, and are established in the present truth.*

So many errors in the Body of Christ come from men and women who got bored with the truth and sought to teach "new revelations". There is no time more dangerous to the spiritual health of a church as when the leadership decides to introduce "new ideas". Paul strictly warned Timothy to avoid this!

1 Timothy 1
3 As I besought you to abide still at Ephesus, when I went into Macedonia, that you might charge some that they teach no other doctrine,
4 Neither give heed to myths and endless genealogies, which cause questions, rather than godly edifying which is in faith: so do.
5 Now the end of the commandment is love out of a pure heart, and of a good conscience, and of faith unfeigned:
6 From which some having swerved have turned aside unto vain talk;

Perhaps you will agree with Paul, that many churches are more known for their vain jangling (noise-making) than for love out of a pure heart and sincere faith in the lives of the members! He seemed to have been speaking about Christianity in our day when he wrote this.

This concept is borne out even in natural situations.

In most cultures, people do not eat the same meal every day. There is often some variety to the food, except for extremely poor homes. Yet, even in the homes of the very rich, this variety is often not that much. Most people find that a little variety in the same old meals on a day-to-day basis works best for them. It isn't having a wide variety in the food you eat on a day-to-day basis that causes you to receive nourishment and strength from it.

I wouldn't want to have my pastor preach the same sermon every Sunday for donkey's years, but I know from the Bible that it would be a disaster if he doesn't repeat many of his sermons often. That is actually the best spiritual diet for me.

Many well-meaning Bible reading plans try to have the readers go through all 66 books in one year. Sometimes, they make them go through all 66 books in two years. Perhaps a better Bible reading plan would help us to focus on the foundations of the faith, and go through them **many times** in a year.

To give another illustration, someone who's been driving cars for 20 years doesn't necessarily know or need to know more driving rules than one who's just been driving for a year. He just has 20 years' experience applying the same old rules in what may be more interesting situations, and may be more dexterous in managing challenging scenarios. This is the same way that one who has been a believer for many years will not be better off than a new believer because he knows more of what the Bible teaches, but because he's more experienced in putting what he knows into practice.

Never let it seem like too much of a burden for you to remind the saints of things that you know they already know. We have placed a lot of emphasis on the special programmes where a "big man of God" will come and teach some new doctrine "that will change your life forever". But this is not really the Biblical pattern.

1 Timothy 4
16 Take heed unto yourself, and unto the doctrine; **continue in them***: for in doing this you shall both save yourself, and them that hear you.*

2 Timothy 3
14 But **continue in the things which you have learned and have been assured of***, knowing of whom you have learned them;*

Hebrews 2
*1 Therefore **we ought to give the more earnest heed to the things which we have heard**, lest at any time we should let them slip.*

James 1
*25 But whoever looks into the perfect law of liberty, **and continues in it**, he being not a forgetful hearer, but a doer of the work, this man shall be blessed in his deed.*

1 John 2
*7 Brethren, I write **no new commandment** unto you, but an old commandment which you had from the beginning. **The old commandment is the word which you have heard from the beginning.***
*24 Let that therefore abide in you, which you have heard from the beginning. **If that which you have heard from the beginning shall remain in you**, you also shall continue in the Son, and in the Father.*

As a Travailing Father, you will not find it too difficult to remind believers of the truth. You will not use flattering words, or a cloak of covetousness. You will not give up on them easily. People will know that they can take you for granted. People will take you for granted. You will forgive them, and give them another chance. You will be their father who will travail again for them, like a woman giving birth.

6. **The Interceding Priest**

1 Peter 2

5 You also, as living stones, are built up into a spiritual house, a holy priesthood, to offer up spiritual sacrifices, acceptable to God by Jesus Christ.

9 But you are a chosen generation, a royal priesthood, a holy nation, a people for his own; that you should show forth the praises of him who has called you out of darkness into his marvelous light:

Revelation 1

6 And has made us a kingdom and priests unto God and his Father; to him be glory and dominion forever and ever. Amen.

The next metaphor we consider is that of the believer as an interceding priest.

Intercession is prayer, petition, or entreaty in favour of someone else[1]. A priest is one authorised to perform the sacred rites of

1. Merriam-Webster Online Dictionary © 2015 Merriam-Webster, Inc.

a religion especially as a mediatory agent between humans and God[2].

In the Old Testament, the nation of Israel had priests, who were meant to act as intermediaries between God and the rest of the people. To be a priest in the Old Testament, one must have been descended from Aaron, who was the older brother of Moses and who was appointed as Israel's first High Priest. His sons were also consecrated as priests, and all subsequent priests descended from them.

Peter says that as believers we constitute "a holy priesthood", and that we are "living stones" that are being used to build "a spiritual house". These are extremely important concepts to understand.

Living Stones – A Spiritual House

First, the Spirit of God writing through Peter calls us "living stones". We are like the stones being used to build a house, with the difference that we are alive, and the house we are being used to build is a "spiritual house".

Think about it. All other things being equal, none of the stones on a construction site is particularly useful or valuable. No one would go to a construction site and say to the foreman, "Oh what a lovely brick! Could you allow me to keep this one for my collection of bricks?" The stones are there, and are only useful and valuable because they contribute to the building at large, and they provide support to each other to be able to do that.

As believers, we make up a "spiritual house", and as "living stones" we provide support to one another to be able to make up the

2. Merriam-Webster Online Dictionary © 2015 Merriam-Webster, Inc.

house. No stone by itself, no matter how important, makes up the house by itself. Most of the stones will depend on the support of stones below them, and will themselves support stones above them. This principle is very important in appreciating our role as "a holy priesthood".

Jesus is Our High Priest

To understand our role as priests, we must also understand the role of Jesus as our High Priest.

Hebrews 3
1 Therefore, holy brethren, partakers of the heavenly calling, consider the Apostle and High Priest of our profession, Christ Jesus;

Hebrews 5
1 For every high priest taken from among men is ordained for men in things pertaining to God, that he may offer both gifts and sacrifices for sins:
4 And no man takes this honor unto himself, but he that is called of God, as was Aaron.

1 Timothy 2
5 For there is one God, and one mediator between God and men, the man Christ Jesus;
6 Who gave himself a ransom for all, this to be a testimony at the proper time.

In the same way that Aaron was the pioneer of a dynasty of priests in the Old Covenant, Jesus became the pioneer of a dynasty of priests in the New Covenant. Aaron offered bulls and goats in sacrifice and his descendants continued this practice, but Jesus offered Himself as a perfect sacrifice once and for all.

Hebrews 10

8 Above when he said, Sacrifice and offering and burnt offerings and offering for sin you desired not, neither had pleasure in them; which are offered by the law;

9 Then said he, Lo, I come to do your will, O God. He takes away the first, that he may establish the second.

10 By the which will we are sanctified through the offering of the body of Jesus Christ once for all.

11 And every priest stands daily ministering and offering frequently the same sacrifices, which can never take away sins:

12 But this man, after he had offered one sacrifice for sins forever, sat down on the right hand of God;

13 From then on waiting till his enemies be made his footstool.

14 For by one offering he has perfected forever them that are sanctified.

Aaron and his descendants must have sacrificed a whole lot of bulls and goats in their day. But Jesus, in His function as a High Priest has only offered a single sacrifice, the sacrifice of Himself. Jesus the High Priest sacrificed Jesus the Lamb of God! What a divinely orchestrated act of Eternal Love! This sacrifice was so perfect, so appropriate, so fitting to the requirements that He has never needed to offer any other blood since then. His own blood will avail for all time!

Our Present-Day Ministry

Well then, what work is left for us to do as priests? Jesus has offered the perfect sacrifice; we don't have to shed any more blood like the descendants of Aaron. Our role as priests is now confined to two activities: giving praise and thanksgiving to God on behalf of others, and praying on behalf of others. This praying for others is what is called intercession.

We Offer Praise and Thanksgiving

In the Old Testament, the priests gave praise and thanks to God for the nation of Israel.

2 Chronicles 7
6 And the priests stood at their posts: the Levites also with instruments of music of the LORD, which David the king had made to praise the LORD, because his mercy endures forever, whenever David offered praise by their ministry; and the priests sounded trumpets opposite them, and all Israel stood.

2 Chronicles 31
2 And Hezekiah appointed the divisions of the priests and the Levites according to their divisions, every man according to his service, the priests and Levites for burnt offerings and for peace offerings, to minister, and to give thanks, and to praise in the gates of the camp of the LORD.

In the New Testament, we are also priests who give praise and thanks to God. In fact, Jesus taught that God was dissatisfied with the worship of the Old Testament and that He sought those who would worship Him in spirit and in truth. That's referring to us!

John 4
23 But the hour comes, and now is, when the true worshipers shall worship the Father in spirit and in truth: for the Father seeks such to worship him.
24 God is a Spirit: and they that worship him must worship him in spirit and in truth.

Philippians 3
3 For we are the circumcision, who worship God in the spirit, and rejoice in Christ Jesus, and have no confidence in the flesh.

Hebrews 13

11 For the bodies of those animals, whose blood is brought into the sanctuary by the high priest for sin, are burned outside the camp.

12 Therefore Jesus also, that he might sanctify the people with his own blood, suffered outside the gate.

13 Let us go forth therefore unto him outside the camp, bearing his reproach.

14 For here have we no continuing city, but we seek one to come.

*15 By him therefore let us offer the sacrifice of praise to God **continually**, that is, the fruit of our lips giving thanks to his name.*

As New Testament priests our lives should be characterised by continual, ceaseless praise and thanksgiving to God. When we fall into the habit of only doing this when attending a service at church, we lose the essence of New Testament worship, and suggest we're looking back to Old Testament worship, which revolved around the Temple.

We Give Thanks to God for Others

A casual study of Paul's letters shows that a great deal of his thanksgiving involved giving thanks to God for other believers. This should be our preoccupation as well.

1 Corinthians 1

*4 I thank my God always **on your behalf**, for the grace of God which is given you by Jesus Christ;*

Ephesians 1

15 Therefore I also, after I heard of your faith in the Lord Jesus, and love unto all the saints,

*16 Cease not to give thanks **for you**, making mention of you in my prayers;*

Philippians 1
*3 I thank my God upon every remembrance **of you**,*

Philemon 1
*4 I thank my God, **making mention of you always** in my prayers,*

We Stand in Intercession for Others

1 Timothy 2
*1 I exhort therefore, that, first of all, **supplications**, **prayers**, **intercessions**, and **giving of thanks**, be made for all men;*

A study of the prayer life of Paul (based on his own testimony in his epistles) reveals that he spent a great deal of his time praying for others, and he especially craved the prayers of others.

Paul Prayed for Others

Ephesians 1
15 Therefore I also, after I heard of your faith in the Lord Jesus, and love unto all the saints,
*16 Cease not to give thanks for you, **making mention of you in my prayers**;*

Philippians 1
3 I thank my God upon every remembrance of you,
*4 Always **in every prayer of mine for you all making request with joy**,*

Colossians 1
*9 For this cause we also, since the day we heard it, **do not cease to pray for you**, and to desire that ye might be filled with the knowledge of his will in all wisdom and spiritual understanding;*

2 Timothy 1
*3 I thank God, whom I serve from my forefathers with pure con-science, that without ceasing **I have remembrance of thee in my prayers night and day**;*

Paul celebrated those who prayed for others.

Colossians 4
*12 Epaphras, who is one of you, a servant of Christ, greets you, **always laboring fervently for you in prayers**, that you may stand perfect and complete in all the will of God.*

Paul Craved the Prayers of Others

Romans 15
29 And I am sure that, when I come unto you, I shall come in the full-ness of the blessing of the gospel of Christ.
*30 Now I beseech you, brethren, for the Lord Jesus Christ's sake, and for the love of the Spirit, **that you strive together with me in your prayers to God for me**;*
31 That I may be delivered from them that do not believe in Judea; and that my service which I have for Jerusalem may be accepted of the saints;
32 That I may come unto you with joy by the will of God, and may with you be refreshed.

Ephesians 6
*18 **Praying always** with all prayer and supplication in the Spirit, and watching thus with all perseverance and supplication for all saints;*
*19 **And for me**, that utterance may be given unto me, that I may open my mouth boldly, to make known the mystery of the gospel,*

Philippians 1
*19 For I know that this shall turn to my salvation **through your** **prayer**, and the supply of the Spirit of Jesus Christ,*

Colossians 4
2 Continue in prayer, and watch in it with thanksgiving;
*3 **Praying also for us**, that God would open unto us a door of utter-ance, to speak the mystery of Christ, for which I am also in bonds:*
4 That I may make it manifest, as I ought to speak.

1 Thessalonians 5
*25 Brethren, **pray for us**.*

2 Thessalonians 3
*1 Finally, brethren, **pray for us**, that the word of the Lord may have free course, and be glorified, even as it is with you:*

Hebrews 13
*18 **Pray for us**: for we trust we have a good conscience, in all things willing to live honestly.*
*19 But **I beseech you rather to do this**, that I may be restored to you the sooner.*

What is the Purpose of Intercessory Prayer?

As believers, we are never truly independent of one another. Together, we are the living stones that make up one Spiritual House. Together, we are the many members that make up one Body. We need each other, and part of this need, is the need to have others praying for us.

Colossians 4
12 Epaphras, who is one of you, a servant of Christ, greets you,

always laboring fervently for you in prayers, that you may stand perfect and complete in all the will of God.

I know a beloved brother who declared years ago that the prayers of Epaphras were useless because "one believer's prayers cannot make others to stand perfect and entire in all the will of God". This man has moved on from this and other errors, to eventually renouncing his Christian faith. My fond hope and fervent prayer for him is that he would soon be restored to the faith he once heralded.

Paul and Epaphras certainly believed that such prayers were of great value. Paul believed that the prayers of the Romans would deliver him from "them that do not believe in Judaea", and would cause his "service which he had for Jerusalem to be accepted by the saints, and would let him "come unto the Romans with joy by the will of God"[3]. Paul believed that the prayers of the Ephesians would help him to receive utterance and preach the gospel boldly[4]. Paul believed that the prayers of the Colossians would help him to receive utterance, so that he could preach the gospel as he ought to speak[5]. Paul believed that the prayers of the Thessalonians would cause the word of the Lord to have free course, and be glorified[6]. The writer of the Letter to the Hebrews believed that the prayers of his audience would cause him to be released from prison much earlier than one would ordinarily expect[7].

Some believers who have disdained the intercessory prayers of the saints have struggled for years. Some have trusted in their great

3. Romans 15:29-32
4. Ephesians 6:18,19
5. Colossians 4:2-4
6. 2 Thessalonians 3:1
7. Hebrews 13:18,19

gifts and abilities only to find that they are not enough. I even know some who said, "I do not need your prayers. I do not need you to pray for me. Please don't pray for me." We may not be sure of their reason for saying this, but we can be sure that such attitudes are strange to the gospel of our Lord Jesus Christ, and are a manifestation of rebellion against the authority of the apostles of Christ Jesus.

James 4

6 But he gives more grace. Therefore he says, God resists the proud, but gives grace unto the humble.

1 Peter 5

5 Likewise, you younger, submit yourselves unto the elder. Yea, all of you be subject one to another, and be clothed with humility: for God resists the proud, and gives grace to the humble.

When you grow up, you will take your place as an Intercessory Priest. You will pray for others and they will pray for you. Together we will do great things in His Service!

7. **The Vessel unto Honour**

2 Timothy 2

19 Nevertheless the foundation of God stands sure, having this seal, The Lord knows them that are his. And, Let every one that names the name of Christ depart from iniquity.

20 But in a great house there are not only vessels of gold and of silver, but also of wood and of earth; and some to honor, and some to dishonor.

*21 If a man therefore purge himself from these, **he shall be a vessel unto honor**, sanctified, and fit for the master's use, and prepared unto every good work.*

One of the ways by which Christians in America have influenced Christianity in Nigeria has been in the area of the songs that we sing. Quite a lot of our hymns and contemporary songs have been imported wholesale from the United States. Some of these songs become quite popular and endure for years on end, others are discarded after a few years.

Here's a chorus we used to sing back in the day.

If You can use anything Lord,
You can use me,
If You can use anything Lord,
You can use me,
Take my hands, Lord,
And my feet,
Touch my heart, Lord,
Speak through me,
If You can use anything Lord,
You can use me.[1]

Can God use anything? **Yes!** Does He want to use you? **Yes!** Do you want Him to use you the way you are? **Probably not.**

Using a household as an illustration, Paul observes that there are typically many vessels, or containers in it. The people living in the house use all of them, but not for the same purposes. I don't know how you run your home, but I assume you don't take your dinner from the same bowl that your dog or cat uses. Even if it were a brand-new never-been-used bowl for feeding pets, you probably would prefer not to use it. You would probably prefer a very old dinner plate to a brand-new dog bowl.

God wants to use us, but He would prefer to use us for noble purposes.

2 Timothy 2
20 But in a great house there are not only vessels of gold and of silver,

1. *Written by Dewitt Jones and Ron Kenoly. © 1993 Deinde Music/Integrity's Praise! Music*

but also of wood and of earth; and **some to honor,** *and* **some to dis-**
honor.

Reading through the Bible, we see God used all sorts of people, and all sorts of things. In the Old Testament, He once used a donkey to talk to someone[2]. Today, some folks become proud because they are great preachers, causing us to conclude that God is still in the business of talking through donkeys!

In the hands of Moses, an ordinary shepherd's rod became a sceptre to break the might of Egypt. In the hands of David, five smooth stones became missiles to destroy a blasphemous giant. In the Bible, God has used pagans and prostitutes, murderers and drunkards, swindlers and thieves, tyrants and false prophets, and other people of similarly dubious vocation.

A Vessel unto Dishonour

God used many people in the Bible for purposes that weren't in their own best interests.

Acts 1
16 Men and brethren, **this scripture must needs have been ful-**
filled, *which the Holy Ghost by the mouth of David spoke before concerning Judas, which was guide to them that took Jesus.*
17 For he was numbered with us, and had obtained part of this ministry.

It had been prophesied that Jesus would be betrayed, so definitely someone had to have that job. You wouldn't have volunteered for it, would you?

2. Numbers 22:28,30

Genesis 15

*13 And he said unto Abram, **Know of a surety** that your descendants shall be sojourners in a land that is not theirs, and shall serve them; and they shall afflict them four hundred years;*
*14 And also that nation, whom they shall serve, **will I judge**: and afterward shall they come out with great possessions.*

It had also been prophesied that the Israelites would be slaves in some foreign land and that their masters would suffer God's judgement before the Israelites would leave with their wealth. Don't you feel somewhat sorry for the Egyptians?

God uses some people **in spite of themselves**. Where He needs a greedy and unfaithful man to betray Jesus, Judas will show up. God didn't make Judas a traitor so he could betray Jesus, He found a traitor who was willing to take the job. Where He needs a cruel tyrant to oppress the Israelites, the Pharaoh of Egypt will prove to be just like that, and a very proud and stubborn one, too. Where He needs a man who will engage in some sort of devilry, there will always be someone available to further His divine agenda.

Romans 3

5 But if our unrighteousness commends the righteousness of God, what shall we say? Is God unrighteous who takes vengeance? (I speak as a man)
6 God forbid: for then how shall God judge the world?
7 For if the truth of God has more abounded through my lie unto his glory; why yet am I also judged as a sinner?
8 And not rather, (as we are slanderously reported, and as some affirm that we say,) Let us do evil, that good may come? whose condemnation is just.

This is what it means to be a vessel unto dishonour.

A Vessel unto Honour

Sometimes God needs some man or woman to fit some noble purpose. It almost always turns out that, by His grace, they've prepared themselves to be fit for such a purpose.

Isaiah 7
14 Therefore the Lord himself shall give you a sign; Behold, a virgin shall conceive, and bear a son, and shall call his name Immanuel.

There must have been many young ladies who preserved their sexual purity until they got married, but only one was chosen to be the mother of Jesus. If Mary had not met this requirement, her place would no doubt have gone to another.

If Any Man Purge Himself

It is no particular distinction to be able to say God uses you. He'll use anyone and anything to further His agenda as He sees fit. What you really want, is for Him to use you for higher purposes. If He's the householder, you want to be His dinner set, not His slop jar.

There have been many who can see God using them, even for godly purposes, and have not realised that He is using them only to the extent that He can. For example, if God wants you to start a church in some city but you do so in another city, it doesn't mean no one will be blessed by your ministry, even though you are in disobedience. Men and women could give multiple testimonies about how God has used you to bless them! Some will get saved, meet their spouses and raise godly families in that church! But there will be the "small matter" of judgement to come, though.

1 Corinthians 4

*3 But with me it is a very small thing that I should be judged of you, or of man's judgment: yea, **I judge not my own self**.*

4 For I know nothing against myself; yet am I not thereby justified: but he that judges me is the Lord.

*5 Therefore **judge nothing before the time**, until the Lord comes, who both will bring to light the hidden things of darkness, and will make manifest the counsels of the hearts: and then shall every man have praise of God.*

In spite of all his labours and achievements in the ministry, Paul says the One who would judge him properly is the Lord. He's the One who knows the thoughts in our minds when we do the things we do. He's the One who knows whether we acted out of genuine love for Him and His people, or whether we sought to increase our empires while pretending to be advancing the Kingdom of God.

Many times, we celebrate ministers of the gospel and even call them "a blessing to the Body of Christ". But how do we reach our conclusions? If you do not know a soldier's orders, how can you tell if he has executed them faithfully? If you do not know what the question was, how can you decide whether I gave the correct answer? There have been students who failed examinations, not because they didn't write something down that showed a good knowledge of the subject matter, but because they didn't follow the specific instructions given to be used while answering the questions.

2 Timothy 2

4 No man that wars entangles himself with the affairs of this life; that he may please him who has chosen him to be a soldier.

5 And if a man also competes as an athlete, yet is he not crowned, unless he strives lawfully.

It is easy enough to know when a minister has deviated from the truth as revealed in Scripture and is walking in error. It is much harder to conclude that he has spent his life obeying God. Paul declares that he doesn't even judge himself!

We will stand before God's throne to give an account of our Christian service, and the Lord will ask some, "Do you admit that while people were praising you for your years of service, in your heart you knew you were walking in disobedience?"

Well, how can you make sure you're a vessel to honour, and not a vessel to dishonour? Paul is very clear. He asks you to purge yourself. Simply purge yourself of the things that defile.

1 Timothy 4
1 Now the Spirit speaks expressly, that in the latter times some shall depart from the faith, giving heed to deceitful spirits, and doctrines of demons;
2 Speaking lies in hypocrisy; having their conscience seared with a hot iron;

2 Timothy 3
1 This know also, that in the last days perilous times shall come.
2 For men shall be lovers of their own selves, covetous, boasters, proud, blasphemers, disobedient to parents, unthankful, unholy,
3 Without natural affection, truce breakers, false accusers, incontinent, fierce, despisers of those that are good,
4 Traitors, reckless, conceited, lovers of pleasures more than lovers of God;

Acts 20
29 For I know this, that after my departing shall grievous wolves enter in among you, not sparing the flock.

30 Also of your own selves shall men arise, speaking perverse things, to draw away disciples after them.

These men (and women) will be people in the church, not outside it. Sometimes when we read these verses we think they speak about unbelievers, but they actually speak of believers who have "departed from the faith". So, who are the believers through whom these terrible predictions by the Holy Spirit through Paul will be fulfilled?

If you don't purge yourself, you might be one of them. You'll be a vessel unto dishonour.

If you will purge yourself, you won't be one of them. You'll be a vessel unto honour!

8. **Pressing On...**

Philippians 3

7 But what things were gain to me, those I counted loss for Christ.

8 Yea doubtless, and I count all things but loss for the excellency of the knowledge of Christ Jesus my Lord: for whom I have suffered the loss of all things, and do count them but rubbish, that I may win Christ,

9 And be found in him, not having my own righteousness, which is of the law, but that which is through the faith of Christ, the righteousness which is of God by faith:

*10 That I may know **him**, and **the power of his resurrection**, and **the fellowship of his sufferings**, being made conformable unto his death;*

11 If by any means I might attain unto the resurrection of the dead.

12 Not as though I had already attained, either were already perfect: but I follow after, if indeed I may apprehend that for which also I am apprehended of Christ Jesus.

13 Brethren, I count not myself to have apprehended: but this one thing I do, forgetting those things which are behind, and reaching forth unto those things which are before,

14 I press toward the mark for the prize of the high calling of God in

Christ Jesus.

15 Let us therefore, as many as would be perfect, be thus minded: and if in anything you be otherwise minded, God shall reveal even this unto you.

16 Nevertheless, to what we have already attained, let us walk by the same rule, let us mind the same thing.

Of all of Paul's epistles which are a part of the New Testament, the Letter to the Philippians and the Second Letter to Timothy were written last. He wrote both books while he was in prison in Rome, and he suffered martyrdom subsequently. This means that the Letter to the Philippians was written **at the end** of Paul's life and ministry, not in the beginning or in the middle.

Think about it – Paul of Tarsus, the great apostle to the Gentiles[1], who had planted so many churches[2], who had laboured more than all the other apostles[3], who had preached Christ in so many places with mighty signs and wonders[4], who had received an abundance of visions and revelations[5], who had seen our Lord Jesus Christ and been personally taught by Him[6], who had suffered so much persecution and affliction for the sake of the gospel[7] – this man still states so very humbly, **at the end of his ministry**, "Not that … I have now already been brought to that place of absolute spiritual maturity beyond which there is no progress…"[8].

1. Galatians 2:7,8
2. 1 Corinthians 3:6
3. 1 Corinthians 15:10
4. Romans 15:18-19, 2 Corinthians 12:12
5. 2 Corinthians 12:1,7
6. Galatians 1:11,12; 1 Corinthians 9:1; 1 Corinthians 11:23; 1 Corinthians 15:8
7. 2 Corinthians 1:8; 2 Corinthians 11:23-27; Ephesians 3:13; Colossians 1:24
8. Philippians 3:12 (WUEST)

At the end of the life and the ministry of Paul, he desires a deeper knowledge of Jesus Christ. He seeks a deeper knowledge of the power of His resurrection. He wants a deeper knowledge of the fellowship of His sufferings. He assures the Philippians that this is the reason he was "apprehended by Jesus Christ". He was saved to grow and become like Christ.

We will always have a need to keep growing. None of us will ever actually finish "growing up", in the sense that we sometimes use that expression to describe a mature adult. We will never achieve "absolute spiritual maturity" on this side of eternity.

Instead, our goal should be to keep "pressing on", just like Paul. Indeed, he says that our continuous improvement is one of the works which the Spirit of God will keep doing until "the day of Jesus Christ".

Philippians 1
6 Being confident of this very thing, that he who has begun a good work in you will perform it until the day of Jesus Christ:

Philippians 1 (ESV)
6 And so I am sure that God, who began this good work in you, will carry it on until it is finished on the Day of Christ Jesus.

Take Your Place

Our continuous growth is also one of the reasons He gave the ministry offices to the Body of Christ.

Ephesians 4
11 And he gave some, apostles; and some, prophets; and some, evangelists; and some, pastors and teachers;
12 For the perfecting of the saints, for the work of the ministry, for

the edifying of the body of Christ:
13 Till we all come in the unity of the faith, and of the knowledge of the Son of God, unto a perfect man, unto the measure of the stature of the fullness of Christ:
14 That we from now on be no more children, tossed to and fro, and carried about with every wind of doctrine, by the sleight of men, and cunning craftiness, by which they lie in wait to deceive;
15 But speaking the truth in love, may grow up into him in all things, who is the head, even Christ:
*16 From whom the whole body being fitly joined together and knit together by that which every joint supplies, **according to the effectual working in the measure of every part**, makes increase of the body unto the edifying of itself in love.*

Ephesians 4 (ESV)
15 Rather, speaking the truth in love, we are to grow up in every way into him who is the head, into Christ,
*16 from whom the whole body, joined and held together by every joint with which it is equipped, **when each part is working properly**, makes the body grow so that it builds itself up in love.*

Each one of us has an obligation to grow, because a lack of growth on your part or my part isn't just a personal problem. You and I are supposed to grow, partly based on the nourishment we receive from other members of the Body of Christ. In turn, others are supposed to grow, partly based on nourishment they receive from you and me. When an individual member of the Body of Christ doesn't grow, he or she deprives the rest of the Body of the invaluable contribution he or she would have made.

1 Corinthians 12
12 For as the body is one, and has many members, and all the members of that one body, being many, are one body: so also is Christ.

13 For by one Spirit were we all baptized into one body, whether we be Jews or Gentiles, whether we be bond or free; and have been all made to drink into one Spirit.

14 For the body is not one member, but many.

15 If the foot shall say, Because I am not the hand, I am not of the body; is it therefore not of the body?

16 And if the ear shall say, Because I am not the eye, I am not of the body; is it therefore not of the body?

17 If the whole body were an eye, where would be the hearing? If the whole were hearing, where would be the smelling?

18 But now has God set the members every one of them in the body, as it has pleased him.

19 And if they were all one member, where would be the body?

20 But now are they many members, yet but one body.

21 And the eye cannot say unto the hand, I have no need of you: nor again the head to the feet, I have no need of you.

22 Nay, much more those members of the body, which seem to be more feeble, are necessary:

23 And those members of the body, which we think to be less honorable, upon these we bestow more abundant honor; and our less respectable parts have greater respect.

24 For our more respectable parts have no need: but God has arranged the body together, having given more abundant honor to that part which lacked:

25 That there should be no schism in the body; but that the members should have the same care one for another.

26 And whether one member suffers, all the members suffer with it; or one member be honored, all the members rejoice with it.

27 Now you are the body of Christ, and members in particular.

What a great Body we'll be when we all grow up in Him! What feats of faith and labours of love we'll perform in His Name! How the pleasure of the Lord shall prosper in our hands!

I look forward to maturing as a believer! I want to play my part and take my place. I want to receive nourishment from the rest of the Body. I want to contribute nourishment to the rest of the Body.

Do you?